JAZZ
DAY

JAZZ DAY

THE MAKING OF A FAMOUS PHOTOGRAPH

ROXANE ORGILL

ILLUSTRATED BY
FRANCIS VALLEJO

CANDLEWICK PRESS

First paperback edition 2019

Library of Congress Catalog Card Number 2015933243
ISBN 978-0-7636-6954-6 (hardcover)
ISBN 978-1-5362-0563-3 (paperback)

18 19 20 21 22 23 APS 10 9 8 7 6 5 4 3 2 1

Printed in Humen, Dongguan, China

This book was typeset in Futura.
The illustrations were done in acrylic and pastel.

Candlewick Press
99 Dover Street
Somerville, Massachusetts 02144

visit us at www.candlewick.com

To Patty, Lucy, Erika, and Liz
R. O.

For Mom, Dad, and Laura. Also for Akira—
you were born right when I started this project!
F. V.

Contents

Introduction ix

The Poems 1

Author's Note 43

Biographies 45

Harlem 1958: Beyond Esquire. 52

Source Notes 53

Bibliography 54

Introduction

In 1958, Art Kane had a crazy idea. Gather as many jazz musicians as possible in one place for a big black-and-white photograph, like a kind of graduation picture. Kane was a graphic designer and a jazz buff, not a photographer. He didn't even own a proper camera. But he pitched the idea to the boss at *Esquire* magazine, and the boss went for it. *Esquire* was planning an issue on American jazz. The music was in an age of glory, with a multitude of brilliant performers and a diverse audience that extended to the far corners of the globe. The photo would be just right for the special supplement, "The Golden Age of Jazz."

Everyone assumed that the photograph would be shot in a studio, where things could be controlled. Kane had a different idea.

He trudged up one Harlem street and down another, surveying entire blocks of tall row houses. It took all day. He was looking for an "absolutely typical brownstone," and he found it on 126th Street between Fifth and Madison Avenues. Number 17, on the north side, would get the light he wanted. He'd line up the musicians with the four-story building in the background.

Kane had *Esquire* call the police department to block the street for a few hours on Tuesday, August 12, so traffic wouldn't interfere with the taking of the photograph. (This picture could take a while to get right.)

He still needed a camera. He borrowed two: a Contax D 35-millimeter and a Hasselblad $2\frac{1}{4}$-by-$2\frac{1}{4}$ inch, which he could set on a tripod.

He had the place, the date, the time, and the equipment, but he had no guarantee of who would come. *Esquire* staff put the word out to Local 802 of the musicians' union, recording studios, music writers, managers, nightclub owners—anyone who had contact with jazz players. The invitation was open to all jazz musicians: a photo shoot, no instruments required. Who would be in New York? Who would be willing and available on Tuesday, August 12? Who would be up before noon after a long night of performing? Jazz people are night people. Who among them would show up at ten *in the morning*?

Early
Art Kane, photographer

nobody here yet
it's only nine
look right
where they come from the train
look left
where they exit a taxi
where to put them all
what if only four come
or five
"The Golden Age of Jazz"
with five guys
look right
look left
a crazy request
what if nobody shows
look up
will it rain
will they wilt
when the sun beats
head out for a cold beer
look right
is that somebody
a group from the train
Lester Young cigarette dangling
that funny squashed hat
man with an umbrella rolled tight
Milt Hinton, hardly know him
without his bass
look left
guy in a striped tie
it's happening

Some Kind of Formation

Hundred-and-twenty-six street
on a Tuesday morning
long-time-no-see
"Hi ya, Monk!"
"Fump, my man!"

camera guy's sweeping
jazzmen like bundles
toward number 17

they don't notice
too busy with how you been

he's shouting
rolling the *Times* into a megaphone
"Please, please get into some kind of formation"

no one listens
musicians
don't hear
words of instruction
only music

So Glad

Milt "Fump" Hinton, bassist and amateur photographer

Walking
Talking
Laughing
Shouting
Standing around
In one big spot
On a long block
At ten in the morning
They're all here
Glad I brought my Leica
And the Canon 35
My little Keystone eight-millimeter too
Gave it to Mona, my wife
"Honey, just aim and press the button"
Drummers in a group
And not talking
Bass players not in a group
And talking
"My man, how you been?"
Chubby, Oscar, Wilbur
"How's your wife and kids?"
Here come the big dogs
Coleman Monk Dizzy Roy
And the beauteous Marian McP
Willie-the-Lion's sitting down
Next to Luckey resting
His cane with the elephant head
They're all here
For some magazine
Me I'm snapping pictures
Lots and lots of pictures
To remember
Later
Forever
So glad

Scuffle

The Boys

Boys on the curb
an even dozen
big and small
one sucked
the two middle fingers
of his right hand
continuously
boys on the curb
waiting for something
to happen

The kid in the lucky spot
next to the man
they called the "Count"
couldn't take his eyes off
shined shoes stark
white shirt cuffs
clean handkerchief
didn't see
little Nelson
who came up
from behind
knocked him
into the man

The kid in the lucky spot
slugged little Nelson
who hit back

Alfred in long trousers
long experience
in settling scuffles
reached in
without fear
yanked the two apart
got a bite on the finger
from Nelson
his little brother

Boys on the curb
an even dozen
big and small
the kid in the lucky spot
drummed an imaginary drum
showing off for the Count
little Nelson clapped his knees
Alfred eyed the guy
fitting camera to tripod
wondered which button you
push
fight forgotten
mood mended
boys

Names
William "Count" Basie, pianist

Nobody calls me Bill
Except my wife
I'm the Count
Ol' Base
Or Holy Main
As in main stem
The buck stops here
Guys in the band
They give you a name
To fit your personality
Or your playing
Same thing
Dizzy
Fump
Stuff
Hawk
Hot Lips
Red
Pee Wee
Pres
Short for President
Of the Tenor Saxophone
Who's Lester Young
Got his name
From Eleanora
Known as Billie Holiday
Except to Pres
Who calls her Lady Day
He calls lots of people Lady
Even me

How to Make a Porkpie Hat
Lester "Pres" Young, tenor saxophonist

Take a tall black hat with a very wide brim,
        punch out the dome.
Roll the crown halfway down all around—
        that's called "busting it down."
Turn it over and poke out the pit just a bit,
        "bringing the lid back home."

And you've got it
a cap
like a padre's
but flatter
with a brim
like a platter
invented
like his sound
as soft as butter
and the way
he spoke in code
a "gray boy" was a white man
a "tribe," a band
Lester played with air between the notes
not like Coleman, who crowded his choruses
Lester wore it pulled down low
his own
perfected
porkpie

Don't Get Me Started
Alfred, a boy

Don't get me started
on her Cadillac
don't let's talk about
tail fins
whitewalls
L-shaped chrome
trim
hooded dash
pan-o-ramic windshield
Imagine the view
"Mary Lou!"*
Greetings all round
for the lady
getting out
of the Caddy
slim ankles
soft skirt
The pink of her blouse is like Easter
They like her better than her car
Ask me
chick or V-8?
No contest:
Cadillac

*Mary Lou Williams, pianist and composer

Late
Thelonious Monk, pianist

The man from the record company hired a taxi
To pick up Thelonious Sphere Monk
Who had a regular gig with a quartet
At the Five Spot in Cooper Square
Turned them away
Night after night
Late
Monk was always late
For work at the Five Spot
Straight to the piano
To play a melody
His quartet could not follow
Did a dance during Johnny Griffin's solo
Or went for a stroll through the club
Six nights a week Mondays off

Ten in the morning was unspeakably early
For Thelonious Sphere Monk
Who was always
Late
Taxi waited outside his building
On West Sixty-Third
Meter running
An hour and more
While Monk tried on jackets
To complete the perfect outfit
Emerging at last in pale-yellow linen
Skinny tie, dark slacks, porkpie hat
And the inevitable bamboo-frame sunglasses
The ones he always wore to play
"Misterioso"

What to Wear (from A to Z)
The Musicians

A dress shirt
Bow tie
Cuff links
Dangling
Earrings
Fedora
Garters gripping socks
Handkerchiefs
In
Jacket pockets
Khaki trousers
Leather loafers
Mostly sport coats

Nylon stockings
One bolo tie
Panama hats of
un**Q**uestionable taste
Regimental
Striped
Ties
Umbrella, unopened
V-necked dress in white
Wing tips
e**X**posed sock of Count Basie
Yellow linen
ja**Z**zy threads

Hat
Alfred, a boy

Nice wool felt
Two-inch snap
Brim
Count's too beat
To give chase
When
Nelson nabs
His bonnet
I'm
On it quick
Down the block

                "Hand it over, Nelson, before I—"

Buff the felt
Set the snap
Brim
"Your hat, Count Basie."

The Invitation Said No Instruments
Rex Stewart, cornetist

Rex unzipped his carrying case
Drawing Leroy like a moth
To the light of the silver cornet
Leroy in short pants
Shoes untied
"Can I try?"
Lips to mouthpiece
Nothing

Rex grabbed the horn
Growl
All heads on the street
Turned
All recognizing
The particular half-valve subhuman sound
Of Rex Stewart
Who used to play with Duke
A nightly solo with the band
"Boy Meets Horn"
Five long minutes all his own

Leroy again
"Can I try?"
Rex passed the cornet
"Make like you're going to kiss a girl"
Lips to mouthpiece
Squeak
(Leroy's too young for girls)
Rex tucked his horn under his arm
The invitation said no instruments

There's a Hole in the Picture
Duke Ellington, pianist and composer

Where's Duke?
On a cruise?
Not till October
In the studio?
That was last week
(Waxed "Red Carpet"—now, *there's* a gem)
You can't take a picture of jazz
Without Edward Kennedy E.
Man can pen a song
In less than five minutes
On an overnight bus
By the light
Of a match
Where's Duke?
On a string of one-nighters
Caro, Lena, French Lick
Not till Friday
In the middle of a three-night stand
In Milwaukee
Knocking back a whiskey
Make it a beer
Between sets at the Brass Rail
Yes, Milwaukee
Not anywhere near
Here
Hole

She's Here!
Maxine Sullivan, singer

snagged *Your Hit Parade* at twenty-six
"Loch Lomond" put her on the high road

"I'll be in Scotland before ye"
(imagine a black girl singing that)

got in with a good band
warbling on the radio

chantoosing in the clubs
all that was years ago

she took a side road
happy working as a nurse

a daughter and husband number four
two-story house in the Bronx

they say she's learning valve trombone
but she's here!

come to hang with the cats
reminding all us bass players

and pianists who kept time
on all her records, tours

doll doesn't even make five feet
when she raises her pretty chin

to sing how she "ain't misbehavin',
happy on the shelf, savin' her love"

reminding us all
how much we miss her

At the Window
A girl

Leaning
on elbows
Twirling
a twist
of curly hair
Looking down
on panama crowns
and bald spots
funeral suits
and two-tone shoes
Wishing
at the window
to be old enough
to be down there
with the big kids
Waiting
for the camera guy
to go away
and give back
the street
free the concrete
for stickball
stoopball
anyball

This Moment
Eddie Locke, drummer

Lucky I was home from the road
Saw the notice in the union hall
This moment won't happen again
Calling all jazz cats—no pay

Saw the notice in the union hall
Must be the youngest one here
Calling all jazz cats—no pay
Guys I've heard stories about

Must be the youngest one here
Guys whose names I forgot
Guys I've heard stories about
Ex-boppers from Minton's uptown

Guys whose names I forgot
N'Orleans wailers, masters of stride
Ex-boppers from Minton's uptown
Isn't that Sonny Greer

N'Orleans wailers, masters of stride
Glad to see Luckey's still here
Isn't that Sonny Greer
Thelonious late as usual

Glad to see Luckey's still here
Who's chatting up Mary Lou?
Thelonious late as usual
Ol' Rex looks ready to blow

Who's chatting up Mary Lou?
Rush is all set to warble
Ol' Rex looks ready to blow
What if we started to jam

Rush is all set to warble
Pres with his ax unboxed
What if we started to jam
Just happened to bring my tom

Lucky I was home from the road
Lucky I was free until two
It's jam now or never, brethren
This moment won't happen again

quartet
Dizzy Gillespie, Roy Eldridge, trumpeters
J.C. Heard, drummer
Gerry Mulligan, baritone saxophonist

in the far right corner
dizzy g. and roy e.
trumpet kings
rivals clowning
for j.c. heard
drummer on demand
back from japan
on his shoulder
the hand
of gerry mulligan
young turk
on cool baritone
towering
like a pale ghost
above a dark sea

four men
four styles
standing
like points
on a rhombus
an unlikely quartet
formed
for no other reason
than this photograph
no composer
would ever score
for it
yet
a quartet

Tempo
Willie "the Lion" Smith, pianist

Willie "the Lion" was not up to tempo
The day of the photo shoot
The composer of "Fingerbuster"
Went to sit down holding
His cane with the elephant head
His hat at the usual jaunty angle
Still chomping on a cigar
The Lion rested his paws

Luckey Roberts wandered over
Short and stubby sat with
Tall and lean, remembering
How they bumped up the tempo
For the cats who came after
Pounding left hands
In a finger stretch known as "stride"
William Henry Joseph Bonaparte Bertholoff Smith
Had the longer name
Luckey the bigger hands
A span of fourteen notes—imagine

Willie unwrapped a fresh Corona
Luckey went back to the shoot
The Lion languished on the step
Missed the picture altogether

Some Kind of Formation, Please!

Hundred-and-twenty-six street
on a Tuesday morning
long-time-no-see
"Hi ya, Monk!"
"Fump, my man!"

camera guy's screaming
"Some kind of formation, please!"
a plea so desperate
it's melodic

shuffle
climb the stoop
fan   out   on   the   sidewalk
talk-laugh-roar
smoke-slap-turn
little by little
fifty-seven musicians
form an upside-down T
underlined
by twelve boys
just happen to be sitting on the curb

click
all eyes looking
this way
click
click
it has to be perfect
for *Esquire*

Dizzy sticks out his tongue

‹ click

"The Golden Age of Jazz"

The cover's cerulean
For the special supplement
Esquire, January 1959
Inside, the big picture:
Fifty-seven musicians
All living, all gathered
In black and white
A long August morning
Stretched into afternoon
Fifty-seven musicians
Standing on a stoop
Spilling on the sidewalk
Still talking
Can you hear the music
Window street brownstone
No sky
Although the sky
Was in fact cerulean
That day

Esquire, 60 Cents
Alfred, a boy

A dozen nickels saved
A month of matinees
Missed
And there I am
Alfred
In the bottom row
In my suspenders
Next to Nelson and the Count
Holding on to his hat
Leroy in short pants
And the other boys
A whole lot of men
And three women
In their Sunday best
Me, Alfred
With a patch on my knees
But jeez
I'm in a magazine

You
A Praise Poem for Art Kane

You got there early and wondered if anyone would show up. They did, like some big happy class reunion. You begged them to get into position. Some listened. Most didn't. You felt alone.

Unexpectedly they began to move, slowly, at your command.

You didn't tell anybody where to stand, or how. You didn't shoo away the boys who perched on the curb at the bottom of your picture frame. You didn't tell weary Count Basie to get up and stand with the rest. When the old guy they called "the Lion" wandered off, you let him be. You didn't get annoyed at Dizzy, clowning. Or at Rex, blowing his horn. You waited. You watched. You trusted. You.

Author's Note

The poems in this collection were all inspired by Art Kane's photograph *Harlem 1958*. The verses about the musicians are based on fact. Lester Young, for example, was very particular about his clothing and always well dressed. He explained his method for reconstructing a hat in a photo essay, "How to Make a Pork Pie Hat," in *Ebony* magazine in 1949. Willie "the Lion" Smith missed being in the photo when he sat down next door, where he was briefly joined by his friend Luckey Roberts; the moment was captured in one of the extra photos by Art Kane that can be seen in the book *The Great Jazz Day*.

Kane was by all accounts a wonderful storyteller, but one who did not always adhere to the facts. With the help of his son Jonathan Kane, I tried to set the story of the photograph straight. Contrary to most reports, Kane was not working at *Seventeen* magazine when he pitched an idea for a photograph to the boss at *Esquire*. He had moved on to another job as art director at an advertising agency. He did borrow and use two cameras, and *Harlem 1958* was shot with the Contax 35-millimeter.

The photo took four or five hours to get, so there was time for the neighborhood boys hanging around to get into mischief. They are lined up, sitting on the curb, in the final photo. Their identities are mostly unknown, but sitting with them is Taft Jordan Jr., son of trumpeter Taft Jordan, who's in the photo as well. Taft Jr. is at the end on the right. According to the documentary film, Taft got into a fight with the kid next to him. A boy named Nelson grabbed Count Basie's hat, and another boy took a turn on Rex Stewart's cornet. I used these incidents as departure points. For instance, I gave the boy in suspenders a name, Alfred, and a role in the events, and I had him note the fictionalized arrival of pianist Mary Lou Williams in a Cadillac. And "the kid in the lucky spot" (next to Count Basie) in the poem "Waiting for Something to Happen" is Taft.

One of the beauties of *Harlem 1958* is that not all of the fifty-seven musicians were famous. Dizzy Gillespie and Count Basie were known around the world, of course, but Eddie Locke was just starting out and as yet unknown, even to many in the picture. Others were veteran sidemen, familiar to almost everybody there but not to the general public.

The photograph is also intriguing for the absence of some of the "greats." Why wasn't Duke Ellington present? With the help of Ken Vail's excellent book *Duke's Diary*, I pinned him to Milwaukee, Wisconsin, and learned his itinerary the days before and after. Thus Duke was able, by an author's sleight of hand, to be present—or at least accounted for—on August 12, 1958.

I've known of Art Kane's photograph for about as long as I've been listening to jazz, which I got to know as a sideline to my job as a classical music critic. I've seen the documentary at least three times. I marveled that musicians would show up for a group photo in such great numbers and that they would be having such a good time, as is obvious in the expressions on their faces. I wanted to tell the story of how the photo got made and of some of the people who happened to be in it. What I didn't expect was that I'd begin writing poems. I write prose, not poetry. But *this* story demanded a sense of freedom, an intensity, and a conciseness that prose could not provide. Some poems popped out easily and nearly complete, others had to be reworked a thousand times. While most of the text is free verse, there is some formal poetry, including a pantoum ("This Moment").

I hope the poems contain the sound of jazz music. I hope they send the reader scurrying to listen to recorded or live jazz, without which there would be no *Harlem 1958*.

1. Hilton Jefferson 2. Benny Golson 3. Art Farmer 4. Wilbur Ware 5. Art Blakey 6. Chubby Jackson 7. Johnny Griffin 8. Dickie Wells 9. Buck Clayton 10. Taft Jordon 11. Zutty Singleton 12. Red Allen 13. Tyree Glenn 14. Miff Mole 15. Sonny Greer 16. Jay C. Higginbotham 17. Jimmy Jones 18. Charles Mingus 19. Jo Jones 20. Gene Krupa 21. Max Kaminsky 22. George Wettling 23. Bud Freeman 24. Pee Wee Russell 25. Ernie Wilkins 26. Buster Bailey 27. Osie Johnson 28. Gigi Gryce 29. Hank Jones 30. Eddie Locke 31. Horace Silver 32. Luckey Roberts 33. Maxine Sullivan 34. Jimmy Rushing 35. Joe Thomas 36. Scoville Browne 37. Stuff Smith 38. Bill Crump 39. Coleman Hawkins 40. Rudy Powell 41. Oscar Pettiford 42. Sahib Shihab 43. Marian McPartland 44. Sonny Rollins 45. Lawrence Brown 46. Mary Lou Williams 47. Emmett Berry 48. Thelonious Monk 49. Vic Dickenson 50. Milt Hinton 51. Lester Young 52. Rex Stewart 53. J.C. Heard 54. Gerry Mulligan 55. Roy Eldridge 56. Dizzy Gillespie 57. Count Basie 58. Willie "the Lion" Smith (had walked out of frame moments before the picture was taken)

August 12, 1958, 17 E. 126th St., New York, New York

Biographies

In this section, rather than attempt to relate the lives of all fifty-seven musicians included in the photo, I've focused on the people I wrote about in the poems.

At ten, **William "Count" Basie** (1904–1984) played piano for the silent movies in Red Bank, New Jersey. As a young man he joined some touring vaudeville shows, and when he happened to hear the Blue Devils playing "hot" music with breakneck tempos for a local dance, he knew *this* was the kind of music he wanted to make. He joined the Devils and then other Midwest "territory bands." He named himself the "Count" because he figured there was already a Duke Ellington (pianist) and a King Oliver (trumpet player), and he wanted a big-sounding name.

Later Count Basie put together his own band, with a couple of ex-Devils men, in a little joint called the Reno Club in Kansas City. Everybody in the band improvised from a "head" arrangement (music worked out in the head), because no one, not even Basie, could read music. Late one night, the local radio announcer asked the Count the name of the next number. He looked at the clock and said, "One O'Clock Jump," then proceeded to hammer out what became his best-known tune.

In 1938, Basie got a booking at the Famous Door, a tiny New York club with a national radio broadcast. Being heard coast to coast brought him the fame he had aspired to when he took the name Count.

At the time of the photo shoot, Basie was working frequently in Europe, but whenever he returned to New York, he had a regular gig at Birdland, where the marquee would read simply "Basie's back!" He was a master of keeping the band in perfect, irresistible swing while playing surprisingly few notes.

As a child in Pittsburgh, **Roy Eldridge** (1911–1989) wanted to drive a truck like his father, but the dream dissolved after he was given a trumpet. At age eleven, Eldridge practiced the horn eight hours a day. At fourteen, he engaged in "battles" with Rex Stewart, four years older, to see who could play faster and hit more high notes. He studied Louis Armstrong's trumpet style and followed him into Fletcher Henderson's top-rated dance band. Known as "Little Jazz" for his short stature (he was five foot three), Eldridge was an emotional, hugely powerful player who—contrary to the time—was in demand by white bandleaders such as the drummer Gene Krupa (who called him "our spark plug").

Although by the late 1940s, Eldridge's music was considered old-fashioned at home, he found an eager audience in Paris and was able to restart his career. In 1958 he was back in the U.S. and working in small groups, including one with Coleman Hawkins, a tenor saxophonist with a big, aggressive sound (see Lester Young's bio). They made a formidable team. "All my life I've loved to battle. And if they didn't like the look of me and wouldn't invite me up on the bandstand, I'd get my trumpet out by the side of stand and blow at them from there," Eldridge said.

Edward Kennedy "Duke" Ellington (1899–1974) refused piano lessons, preferring to play football, baseball, and other sports as a kid. Hanging around the pool hall in his teenage years, he gravitated to the pianists and began learning from them. He gave himself the nickname "Duke" because he liked to dress well and because it suited his regal manner, which he carried to the point of making his cousins bow and curtsy to him on the steps of his Washington, D.C., home. Duke Ellington joined his first jazz orchestra, the Washingtonians, as pianist in 1923. With Duke as the leader, the group grew from six to fourteen musicians. The way the band played together was as much his "instrument" as the piano. His approach to composing for jazz orchestra was unusual in that he was inspired by and acutely sensitive to the different sounds his players got out of their instruments. Regarded as the most important composer in jazz, he wrote some two thousand works, from three-minute instrumental pieces to one unperformed opera, *Boola*. In August 1958, he was, as the poem says, on the road in the Midwest with some members of his orchestra.

John Birks "Dizzy" Gillespie (1917–1993) played higher, faster, and more accurately than any brass player before him—with virtually no training. Gillespie wanted a trumpet the minute he saw one in the hands of the boy next door in Cheraw, South Carolina. In the 1950s he switched to a trumpet with the tube bent so the bell turned upward, which he said helped him to hear himself better and directed the sound over the heads of his listeners instead of straight at them. When he blew into the mouthpiece, his cheeks distended like a blowfish. He and saxophonist Charlie Parker launched a radically different style called bebop with the tune "Ko-Ko." Marked by sensational speed, complex harmony, and intricate melody, bebop was initially unpopular because it wasn't music one could dance to. Gillespie was also the first to merge American jazz and Cuban rhythms, which he heard in Spanish Harlem, notably in his composition "A Night in Tunisia."

With the upturned horn, puffed-out cheeks, beret, goatee, and spectacles, Gillespie was instantly recognizable around the world. He did two extensive tours sponsored by the U.S. State Department, playing in a big band throughout the Middle East and South America. He was back to leading small groups at the time of the photo.

At age five, **James Charles "J.C." Heard** (1917–1988) was a tap dancer, at eleven he taught himself drums, and by thirteen he was working with local bands in Detroit. He went on to play in the groups of Count Basie, Louis Armstrong, Benny Goodman, and many others, and can be heard on more than 1,100 albums. He was equally at home with big bands and small combos and was recognized equally as a steady timekeeper and a creative soloist. "Unless you know how to phrase, unless you have some ideas about presence, conception, and attitude, then your solos are just going to be a bunch of noise," Heard said. Ever the versatile performer, he spent several years in Japan and Australia working as a drummer, singer, *and* dancer, but was back in New York in 1958.

Milt "Fump" Hinton (1910–2000) was a bassist first and an amateur photographer second, but after his death, he left behind more than 60,000 photographs.

As a child in Chicago, he played violin, cello, and tuba before taking up double bass in the high-school All-City Orchestra. He was a bassist in Cab Calloway's big band in the 1930s and 1940s, where he earned the nickname "Fump" for the sound of his instrument. He spent most of his career as a freelance musician in high demand, especially for recordings.

At the time of the photograph, he had grown tired of constant touring and was working as a staff musician at CBS Television; he was one of the first African-American musicians in the television industry. Later he returned to the freelance bassist's life. Hinton always claimed the bass was a service instrument rather than a solo instrument. "You must be content in the background," he said, "knowing you're holding the whole thing together."

He started taking pictures of his friends so they could look back one day and remember good times. The hobby grew, and soon Hinton was rarely seen *without* his cameras. "For some reason, I felt strongly about using my camera to capture the people and events from the jazz world that I was lucky enough to see," he said.

Growing up in the Bronx, New York, **Art Kane** (1925–1995) was a frequent visitor to the Bronx Zoo. On one visit, he borrowed his father's camera to take his first picture—not of the animals but of a flag atop a flagpole. When he saw the print, he was utterly disappointed: a white rectangle (the sky) bisected by a line (the pole) with a tiny speck at the top (the flag). He didn't touch a camera again for a long time.

When Kane got the assignment from *Esquire,* he was thirty-three, a well-known graphic designer who'd already been art director at *Seventeen,* a magazine for teenage girls, and at an advertising agency. His experience with photography was limited to snapping pictures on weekend outings with friends. Taking a big photograph of fifty-seven jazz musicians changed everything. "I knew from that moment on that this was what I wanted to do with my life," he said. Kane left his advertising job and became a photographer.

Although he was dismayed with his first picture of a flag, he returned again to flags as a subject. Among his flag-related images are one of the British rock band The Who wrapped in the Union Jack and another of an enormous, rippling American flag with a crowd of people gathered on top (they're actually standing on a hill just behind the Stars and Stripes). He said the reason he photographed the flag so often was to get revenge on the machine that had disappointed him when he was twelve. As time went on, Kane's ideas got bolder, and it became more important to control the image. He once took a fashion shot of a woman sitting on the floor in a beautiful black dress beside a slithering python.

Eddie Locke (1930–2009) played on a homemade drum kit until his family in Detroit could afford a real one. Mostly self-taught, he learned by carrying drums for the great Jo Jones (who played with Count Basie), setting up the drums for his idol, and then watching his every move. For most of his career, Locke was the quintessential sideman, the guy who got the call when a drummer was needed for a performance. He worked steadily, though, with two great leaders: saxophonist Coleman Hawkins (Lester Young's early rival) and trumpeter Roy Eldridge, whom he joined the year the photo was taken. Eldridge once rebuked him for playing badly in a nearly deserted club. Locke tried to excuse himself, saying, "There's nobody here, man." Eldridge leaned over the drum set and said, "*I'm here!*" It was a great lesson, Locke said. "Always give your all to the music." Later in life, Locke taught music to elementary-school students in New York.

Thelonious Sphere Monk (1917–1982) was mostly self-taught on the piano — and sometimes played with his elbows. Just out of his teens, he worked all the gigs he could, playing in small combos with anybody and everybody in New York. He also composed music with ear-bending dissonances on the baby grand piano in his mother's apartment. "I compose as it comes, as I hear it," he said.

In 1957, after a long spell of no work, Monk was hired to play in a little New York bar called the Five Spot, on the edge of Skid Row. Young people lined up for blocks six nights a week hoping to snag one of the seventy-six seats in the tiny, red-walled room to hear Monk and his quartet play exploratory harmonies and out-of-bounds rhythms in tunes like "Epistrophy" and "Rhythm-a-Ning." Saxophonist John Coltrane remarked that when playing with Monk, "You have to be awake all the time. You never know exactly what's going to happen."

In the month the photo was taken, Monk recorded his classic album *Misterioso*, live at the Five Spot. But finding steady work was ever a strain for the brilliant, sensitive Monk. In the 1970s he struggled with mental illness and became a recluse, living in the Weehawken, New Jersey, home of his great patroness and friend, the Baroness Pannonica Koenigswarter, and her approximately one hundred cats.

 **Gerry Mulligan** (1927–1996), an Irish-American who favored bold checked jackets, got his start arranging music for the radio in Pittsburgh. He learned the piano and took up saxophone, first alto and then baritone, bringing a light touch to an often heavy-sounding instrument. Around the time the photo was taken, he was very active with his own piano-less quartet, comprised of baritone sax, trumpet, bass, and drums—an innovation at the time. The quartet toured with Duke Ellington, Mulligan's favorite composer, with whom he shared a fascination with trains and railroads. Even more than his playing, Mulligan's contribution to jazz was writing and arranging low-key, "cool"- sounding, intricate music for a variety of ensembles. "I'll always think as an arranger," Mulligan said.

 From the age of five, **Charles "Luckey" Roberts** (1893–1968) was a dancer, juggler, and acrobat. He toured with minstrel acts and was introduced to the piano, which he preferred to tumbling. By 1910 he was living in New York City, where he wrote and produced vaudeville shows and composed many popular tunes, including "Pork and Beans" and "Shoo Fly."

Roberts was a short man (four foot ten) with unusually large hands; between pinkie and thumb, he could span an interval of fourteen notes on the piano. He was known for his "seismic attack" and technical prowess on the keyboard, but music wasn't his whole life: Roberts was also a successful businessman and owned a bar, Luckey's Rendezvous, which featured singing waiters. Living up to his moniker (derived from his middle name, Luckeyth), he survived a serious car crash and two strokes and continued to play almost to his death. He's the oldest person in the photograph, at sixty-five. Although semi-retired, he made an album that year called *Luckey and the Lion,* for which he and Smith recorded their parts in separate sessions.

 Willie "the Lion" Smith (1897–1973) cut a memorable figure at the piano, mumbling to himself, clenching his teeth around a cigar, wearing his hat set at a precise angle. Smith earned his nickname for bravery as an artilleryman with an all-black unit in World War I.

His interest in music was sparked by listening to his mother play the organ at the Baptist church in Newark, New Jersey. As a young man he performed for dances all night long, changing endlessly the key, tempo, and harmonies to suit his insatiable need for variety. When he and Duke Ellington were in their twenties, they engaged in five-hour "cutting contests" of pure improvisation, each man endeavoring to be more original than the other. Ellington said later, in gratitude, "No one could ever play the same again after once hearing the Lion." He was one of the originators (with his friend and competitor, Luckey Roberts) of a rhythmic piano style known as stride because of the wide stretch required of the pounding left hand.

Still active in 1958, he arrived at the photo shoot dressed in a smart suit and bolo tie. But at some point he got tired and sat down next door. Smith can be seen in other photos that Kane took that day, but he missed being in *the* photo, the one chosen to illustrate *Esquire*'s "Golden Age of Jazz."

William "Rex" Stewart (1907–1967) began his musical adventures playing the cornet in a boys' military band in Washington, D.C. Recalling how he felt when he got his first silver cornet, he wrote, "I didn't want to be separated from that horn for even a minute. I took it to school. I slept with it." He idolized the brilliant Louis Armstrong and replaced him in the Fletcher Henderson Orchestra when he was eighteen years old. When Stewart realized he could not match Armstrong's technique, he perfected a half-valve technique (pressing the valve partway for a fuzzier sound) and a hard-blowing style of his own.

Duke Ellington hired him to play in his orchestra in 1934, and Stewart became a star with hits like "Boy Meets Horn," which he co-wrote with Ellington. Stewart spent eleven years with the band and was known forever after as an "Ellingtonian." He expanded his approach with novel effects like bent notes (playing the quarter-tones *between* the notes on a piano) and "talking" and "growling" through the horn. He also ran a farm in New Jersey, wrote a book about jazz, and worked as a disk jockey. Although semi-retired, he was playing and recording with a Fletcher Henderson reunion band when the photograph was taken.

Maxine Sullivan (1911–1987) was singing at a nightclub in Pittsburgh, her first job, when she bought a round-trip train ticket to New York, intending to stay one night (her only night off). Within hours, she met someone who wanted to listen to her sing; within a week, she had landed a job, which was followed by a huge hit record: a swing version of the Scottish folk song "Loch Lomond." (She never used the other half of her train ticket.) Sullivan's stroke of good luck had its downside: she was forever identified with that one song. With a gift for clear diction and a simple delivery, she got roles in two movies, co-hosted a radio show, and enjoyed long-running engagements in top New York clubs.

By the time of the photo shoot, however, Sullivan had left the music scene to raise her daughter. She was working as a teacher's aide, a nurse, and a volunteer serving her community. She returned to music a few years later, singing in a perfectly pitched, relaxed voice and playing the valve trombone and then the smaller flugelhorn in festivals around the world. Sullivan died a few months after making a live recording in Tokyo, where the last song she sang was "Loch Lomond."

 **Mary Lou Williams** (1910–1981) was a rarity for her time: a *female* jazz pianist, composer, and arranger. She taught herself to play the piano and learned the blues from her stepfather, who sang them over and over to her. By fifteen she was on the road full-time, working to help support her ten half-siblings by performing with a band that backed a comedian named Buzzin' Harris. At eighteen Williams joined Andy Kirk's Clouds of Joy, a "hot" band in great demand in Kansas City and beyond. Williams weighed about ninety pounds, but she played with a heavy attack, like people were used to hearing from a man. She supplied the band with five or six new arrangements a week, which she wrote in the car by flashlight, driving between one-nighters.

Williams moved on easily to new styles, playing boogie-woogie when it was all the rage, and later bebop. In 1957 she was baptized a Catholic and thereafter worked hard to balance her music and her faith. At the time of the photo shoot, she ran a thrift shop and used the proceeds to assist down-and-out musicians. She composed pieces with religious themes, including a jazz mass. "I never thought about anything but the music inside me," Williams said.

 **Lester Young** (1909–1959) learned music from his father, who had a family band that toured in carnivals and other shows. In 1934 he joined Count Basie in Kansas City, and Basie featured him in "Lester Leaps In," one of his so-called flag-wavers—tunes designed to get the audience excited and on its feet, dancing. Young had a great rivalry with Coleman Hawkins, whose tenor sound was full and heavy while Young's was light and floating. Hawkins had arrived on the scene before Young, and it took a long time for Young to gain acceptance. But he grew to have almost a cult following, not only for his musical inventiveness but also for his many eccentricities. He believed, for instance, that a butterfly resting on your hand indicated that someone loved you. He spoke in "jive talk," with utterly original phrases like "gray boys" (white men) and "ding dong," which meant that somebody goofed. At the time of the photo, he played rarely and lived in a hotel room across from Birdland. From his window he watched, brooding, as younger players went to work in the club where he'd often performed. He died from alcoholism six months after the picture was taken.

Harlem 1958: Beyond *Esquire*

Harlem 1958 lives on in film, books, and other media. Here is a list of examples that show the reach of the photograph.

A Great Day in Harlem: documentary film (1994). Producer Jean Bach interviewed Art Kane and several of the musicians some thirty years after the photograph was taken. She also used Mona Hinton's home movie made that day. The film was nominated for an Academy Award in 1995. At one point, trumpeter Art Farmer, gazing at the photo, remembers the many friends, colleagues, and idols he encountered on that single summer's day and says, "They are in us, and they will always be alive."

The Great Jazz Day: book by Charles Graham and Dan Morgenstern (2000). Recounts the making of the documentary and Kane's photograph and introduces three dozen *other* photos taken that day by Kane, Milt Hinton (the bassist who brought his cameras), and Mike Lipskin, a fifteen-year-old student of Willie "the Lion" Smith. The book includes remembrances by Kane, Hinton, Dizzy Gillespie, and others; some of their stories found their way into the poems in this book.

Life magazine's *Great Day in Harlem* re-creation photograph (1996). *Life* reunited ten of the twelve surviving musicians and one former boy forty years later. They took their original positions on East 126th Street, leaving many empty spaces. The "former boy" was Taft Jordan Jr., son of trumpeter Taft Jordan.

The Terminal: movie directed by Steven Spielberg (2004). Tom Hanks stars as Viktor Navorski, an eastern European man stranded in John F. Kennedy Airport due to a snafu in U.S. Customs. Viktor carries around a beat-up coffee can containing autographs of fifty-six musicians from the photo. He has come all this way just to get the fifty-seventh and final signature, from saxophonist Benny Golson.

A Great Day in Seattle (2007), *A Great Day in Indy* (Indianapolis), and *A Great Day in Detroit* (both 2008): copycat or "homage" photographs. On these and other occasions, a photo has been set up like *Harlem 1958* to honor jazz musicians in their hometown. In an interview with the author, Art Kane's son Jonathan Kane said, "People not only know and love the image, but it has become almost a national pastime in America to create your own *Great Day in Whatever.*"

Other homages include:

A Great Day on Eldridge Street (2007), celebrating the 120th birthday of a synagogue on New York's Lower East Side with an overflow crowd of klezmer musicians.

The Greatest Day in Hip-Hop History (*XXL* magazine, 1998), capturing more than two hundred hip-hop artists in an extra-wide photo at the same location as *Harlem 1958*.

Source Notes

p. 45: Origin of the Count's nickname: Basie and Murray, p. 17.

p. 45: "our spark plug": Chilton, p. 111.

p. 46: "All my life . . . them from there": Balliett, *American Musicians,* p. 196.

p. 47: "Unless you know . . . bunch of noise": "J.C. Heard."

p. 47: "You must be content . . . whole thing together": Keepnews.

p. 47: "For some reason . . . enough to see": Hinton, Berger, and Maxson, p. 313.

p. 48: "I knew from that moment . . . with my life": Graham and Morgenstern, p. 23.

p. 48: "There's nobody here, man," "*I'm* here!" and "Always give your all to the music": Chilton, p. 269.

p. 48: "I compose as . . . I hear it": van der Bliek, p. 75.

p. 48: "You have to . . . going to happen": Kelley, p. 230.

p. 49: "I'll always think as an arranger": Heckman.

p. 50: "No one could . . . hearing the Lion": Edwards.

p. 50: "I didn't want . . . slept with it": Stewart, p. 23.

p. 51: "I never thought . . . music inside me": Dahl, p. 60.

p. 51: "gray boys" and "ding dong": Delannoy, p. 151.

p. 52: "People not only . . . *Great Day in Whatever*": interview with the author.

Bibliography

Books

Balliett, Whitney. *American Musicians II: Seventy-One Portraits in Jazz.* Jackson, MS: University Press of Mississippi, 2006.

Basie, Count, with Albert Murray. *Good Morning Blues: The Autobiography of Count Basie.* New York: Da Capo, 1995.

Charters, Samuel B., and Leonard Kunstadt. *Jazz: A History of the New York Scene.* New York: Da Capo, 1984.

Chilton, John. *Roy Eldridge, Little Jazz Giant.* New York: Bloomsbury Academic, 2002.

Dahl, Linda. *Stormy Weather: The Music and Lives of a Century of Jazzwomen.* New York: Limelight, 1989.

Delannoy, Luc. *Pres: The Story of Lester Young.* Fayetteville, AR: University of Arkansas Press, 1993.

Gourse, Leslie. *Straight, No Chaser: The Life and Genius of Thelonious Monk.* New York: Schirmer, 1998.

Graham, Charles, and Dan Morgenstern. *The Great Jazz Day.* Emeryville, CA: Woodford Press, 2000.

Hinton, Milt, and David G. Berger. *Bass Line: The Stories and Photographs of Milt Hinton.* Philadelphia: Temple University Press, 1988.

Hinton, Milt, David G. Berger, and Holly Maxson. *Playing the Changes: Milt Hinton's Life in Stories and Photographs.* Nashville: Vanderbilt University Press, 2008.

Kelley, Robin D.G. *Thelonious Monk: The Life and Times of an American Original.* New York: Free Press, 2009.

Korall, Burt. *Drummin' Men: The Heart of Jazz: The Bebop Years.* New York: Oxford University Press, 1990.

Orgill, Roxane. *Dream Lucky: When FDR Was in the White House, Count Basie Was on the Radio, and Everyone Wore a Hat.* New York: Smithsonian Books/Collins, 2008.

Poppy, John. *The Persuasive Image: Art Kane.* New York: Crowell, 1975. Biographic material and many Kane photographs.

Porter, Lewis, ed. *A Lester Young Reader.* Washington, DC: Smithsonian Institution Press, 1991.

Shipton, Alyn. *Groovin' High: The Life of Dizzy Gillespie.* New York: Oxford University Press, 1999.

Stewart, Rex. *Boy Meets Horn.* Ann Arbor: University of Michigan Press, 1991.

Vail, Ken. *Duke's Diary: The Life of Duke Ellington.* Vol. 2, 1950–1974. Lanham, MD: Scarecrow Press, 2002. Ellington's itinerary in detail.

van der Bliek, Rob, ed. *The Thelonious Monk Reader.* New York: Oxford University Press, 2001.

Wakefield, Dan. *New York in the Fifties.* Boston: Houghton Mifflin, 1992.

Articles

Balliett, Whitney. "Harlem Morning." *The New Yorker,* January 23, 1995. Reprinted in Balliett, Whitney. *Collected Works: A Journal of Jazz, 1954–2000.* New York: St. Martin's, 2000. A jazz critic's view of the photograph and the film *A Great Day in Harlem.*

"The Golden Age of Jazz." *Esquire* 51, no. 1 (January 1959): 98–115. Includes the photo *Harlem 1958* in a double-page spread; *Four Giants,* photographs of Louis Armstrong, Duke Ellington, Lester Young, and Charlie Parker's grave by Art Kane; and essays on jazz past, present, and future.

Heckman, Don. "Jazz: Still Fresh: At 67, baritone sax giant Gerry Mulligan." *Los Angeles Times,* March 13, 1994.

"J.C. Heard: One of the Busiest, Swingin'-est Drummers of Classic Jazz." *Modern Drummer,* February 24, 2010.

Keepnews, Peter. "Milt Hinton, Dean of Jazz Bassists, Is Dead at 90." *New York Times,* December 21, 2000.

Young, Lester. "How to Make a Pork Pie Hat." *Ebony* 4, no. 10 (August 1949): 43–44.

Audiovisual Material

Bach, Jean. *A Great Day in Harlem.* Home Vision Entertainment, 1995. DVD. Companion website: http://www.a-great-day-in-harlem.com.

Seven Lively Arts: The Sound of Jazz. CBS Television, 1957. Thirty-two musicians perform in jam sessions; the aural equivalent of the Harlem photograph. Includes (from the photo): Count Basie, Roy Eldridge, Coleman Hawkins, Thelonious Monk, Gerry Mulligan, and Lester Young. Available on YouTube.

Websites

"Art Kane." Art Directors Club website. The Art Kane entry in the club's Hall of Fame. http://www.adcglobal.org/archive/hof/1985/?id=242.

Art Kane website. Features information about the man and his work; includes an interactive version of *Harlem 1958.* http://www.artkane.com.

Cunnifee, Thomas. "*The Sound of Jazz*: An Interactive Essay." Jazz History Online. http://jazzhistoryonline.com/Sound_of_Jazz_1.html.

Edwards, Bill. "William Henry Joseph Bonaparte Bertholf Smith." "Perfessor" Bill Edwards website. http://www.perfessorbill.com/comps/wsmith.shtml.

The Gerry Mulligan Collection. Library of Congress. http://lcweb2.loc.gov/diglib/ihas/html/mulligan/mulligan-home.html.

"Jazz Greats Digital Exhibits." Institute of Jazz Studies, Rutgers, The State University of New Jersey. Comprehensive online exhibits on Count Basie and Mary Lou Williams, among others. http://newarkwww.rutgers.edu/ijs/.

"Jazz Profiles." National Public Radio website. Profiles of notable jazz musicians with recorded music. http://www.npr.org/music/genres/jazz-blues.

Milt Hinton website, created by David G. Berger and Holly Maxson. http://www.milthinton.com.

Thelonious Monk website. http://www.theloniousmonk.com.